Make GOD Proud!

How to Stop Living Below What GOD Intended For You

Mary Jo Wehniainen

Copyright © 2014 Mary Jo Wehniainen

All rights reserved. No part of this publication may be reproduced in whole or in part, or stored in any retrieval system, or transmitted in any form or by any means, electronic, mechanical, photocopying, recording, or otherwise, without written permission of the author.

Disclaimer & Terms of Use

The book was not prepared, approved, licensed or endorsed by any of the owners of the trademarks or brand names referred to in this book. Terms mentioned that are known or believed to be trademarks or service marks have been indicated as such.

The publisher and author make no representations or warranties with respect to the accuracy or completeness of the contents of this work and specifically disclaim all warranties, including without limitation warranties of fitness for a particular purpose.

No warranty may be created or extended or implied by sales or promotional materials. Neither the publisher nor the author shall be liable for damages arising here from.

Any references to various brand name products and services are for information purposes only, and are not intended to suggest endorsement or sponsorship of the author or publisher.

Second Edition

ISBN-13: 978-1986507691

ISBN: 1986507696

Dear Linnea!

GOD bless you! How wonderful to know you're a mom of 5 precious little ones... just like me — even though mine are no longer little!

Dedicated to my Lord and Savior, JESUS CHRIST.

I pray rich blessings on you, Jonathan, and your very beautiful family — I hope this book encourages you, inspires you, and puts a HUGE seed of hope in your spirits! (Share w/ Jonathan too!) MJ ♥

CONTENTS

Acknowledgments	i
Introduction	1
Decision Time	5
GOD is Doing a New Thing!	9
Out With The Old	15
Next-Level Christianity™	29
The U.P.L.I.F.T. Formula™ to Success with GOD	43
Unplug From the Negative	45
Plug In to GOD	48
Listen Intently	52
Immediately Obey	58
Find Your Gift and Focus	63
Talk, Trust and Tune In to Miracles!	68
Get your Buckets Ready!	77
Everybody's Watching	81
Stay Connected!	83
About The Author	85

ACKNOWLEDGMENTS

I am blessed to have so many wonderful people in my life: my precious family, my dear friends, neighbors, coworkers, and new people I meet each and every day.

My life is truly rich and it is my relationship and encounters with each and every one of you that have made me the person I am today. Thank you so much for allowing me the privilege of having you in my life.

INTRODUCTION

Many Christians nowadays are living mediocre lives; way below what GOD has intended for them.

They love GOD and have faith, but they have crummy relationships, they're stressed out, broke all the time, and lead pretty boring lives.

It's time we changed all that!

This book is not written to teach you goal setting, a new prosperity message, or better time management. It's intended to dramatically change your life for the better; from deep within.

This book is for you if you love GOD, but your life isn't working the way you want. You may be struggling on your job, need help with your finances, have frustrating relationships, feel overwhelmed, confused and worn out... and can't seem to find your way out. Or maybe you have a nagging feeling that GOD has more for your life; that feeling is there for a reason – HE DOES!

It doesn't matter what sort of church you attend, or what denomination you are. Whether you were raised Catholic, Baptist, Pentecostal, Lutheran... (or any of the many other religions) if you love GOD, this book is for you!

This book is NOT for you if you're satisfied with the way

things are. It's not for you if you're a Christian theologian who's more concerned about the letter of the law than the principles behind it. It's not for you if you're closed-minded, judgmental, and think you've got everything already figured out. If you think it's wrong to have fun, this book is DEFINITELY not for you!

Whether you're a Christian business owner who just can't seem to break through to a new level of success, a stay-at-home mom who feels isolated and overwhelmed, a parent who knows you need to change the direction your family is headed, or anyone else who's just plain old fed up, this book should be a breath of fresh air! There IS hope for you, and GOD has an amazing plan for YOUR life!

GOD's children should be the happiest, most peaceful, most successful and most prosperous people on the face of this earth! We should be the ones people are begging to hire, leading huge companies, directing box office hits, athletes everyone wants to recruit, people heading up relief organizations and making a HUGE difference in the world.

The tide is changing... GOD is definitely stirring things up and causing HIS children to take on important roles in every aspect of life.

I've written this book because I know firsthand the pain and frustration of living a mediocre life, way below what GOD intended for me.

As a former shy, stay-at-home homeschooling mom of five small children I was always worried about something, stressed to the max and flat broke. I was so broke I bought my kids' clothes at the thrift store and ate donated food from the church.

Until one day, 18 years ago, when GOD stepped in and turned it all around... and my life has never been the same.

I decided to write this book to help YOU break free from the status quo, and so that you would once and for all know the deep, overwhelming peace, freedom and joy that comes from living the life GOD has planned for you all along.

I can hardly wait to hear YOUR amazing story!

Why references to GOD are capitalized

Several years ago, when I visited a synagogue, I learned that people of the Jewish faith will often write GOD as G-D as a sign of deep respect and reverence. Ever since then, in my personal daily scripture writing, I've made it a point to capitalize GOD and all references to HIS name in a similar display of respect, as you'll see throughout the pages of this book.

Mary Jo Wehniainen

DECISION TIME

It was 4 pm on an overcast, bone-chilling Wednesday. My four kids were busy as usual. (Grace hadn't entered the scene yet, she was born the following year.) Becky was driving her blue toy mini-van back and forth along the side of the sofa where I was laying, Mike and Josh were in the other room playing with Legos®, Daniel sleeping in his bouncy seat on my bed.

The loud banging was almost constant as the furnace in the basement worked hard to keep us warm on this dreary winter's day. The kids were oblivious to my true state of mind, inside I was screaming in quiet, unending desperation. I'd just recovered from a third miscarriage and was worn out: mentally, emotionally and physically. The bills were piling up, and so was the laundry, and there was no hope in sight. My days were a dreary existence of homeschooling, changing diapers, and pinching pennies. My daily challenge was how to go to the grocery store with four dollars and figure how to make dinner for a family of six.

I laid my head back and closed my eyes. Reality blurred as I drifted off to sleep, starring in my own glorious dream. I saw myself standing in the kitchen smiling, with the phone up to my ear, credit card in the other hand, ordering pizza. I could almost smell it. "I'll have one pizza with pepperoni and sausage; one with onions, mushrooms and black olives; and one with double cheese, please!"

Suddenly I was jolted awake by the doorbell. The pizzas were here!

I jumped off the sofa, tripped over the toys on the floor, and opened the front door. Nobody there! I slammed it shut. But something was still ringing. Half asleep, I shook my head, turned around, and came to my senses. It was the phone!

I ran to the kitchen, out of breath, and answered the phone. It was my husband.

That phone call changed my life forever…

> *All who see them will acknowledge that they are a people the LORD has blessed!*
>
> Isaiah 61:9b

That's what the Bible says, so I know it's true, but I guarantee if someone were asked to describe in one word what my life was like 18 years ago, they wouldn't have said "blessed!"

In fact, we probably appeared to be exactly the opposite.

We loved GOD, and did our best to live a life that was pleasing to HIM. We went to church, read the Bible, taught our kids at home so we could have a good influence on them, and always tried to do the right thing. We had good intentions, and we were doing the best we knew how to do.

But besides doing our best to do the "right" thing, everything seemed to go wrong. Really, really wrong.

My husband Chuck worked a full time job and did some house painting on the side so I could stay home with our kids. No matter how hard he worked, we never seemed to have enough money to make ends meet.

I'd be in line at the grocery store and watch as the person in front of me unloaded their cart with all sorts of delicious foods:

steaks, veggies, chips, ice cream; everything looked so good to me. And then I'd watch in amazement as they either pulled out their credit card or even cash to pay for it. How I longed to be able to do the same thing. Something as simple as normal grocery shopping was an unaffordable luxury.

I remember how I felt when I had a few extra dollars to spend. I'd go shopping in the "scratch and dent" room of the local health food store. The labels on the bottles were smeared and sticky, but we got some good bargains. I always wondered how it would feel to stroll down the aisles, shopping basket in hand, and just pick out what I wanted, rather than hope that it would somehow appear in the dark and dingy back room full of other people's rejects.

I remember how time consuming (and disgusting) it was to wash our kids' diapers by hand because we couldn't afford the disposable ones.

It was also during that time that we did all our gift shopping at the dollar store, or when there was a 90% off sale at K-Mart after the holidays. Then we'd store away all the items in a box that we'd pick from when we needed a present for someone.

Several times a year there was a big sale at the Lillian Vernon outlet store near our home. They specialize in all sorts of neat toys and gadgets and personalize them so they're truly unique. We got quite a few things there for our kids, at crazy discount prices, but it was always confusing to our kids when we gave them the toys because they had someone else's name inscribed on them.

Through this entire time, we never complained. What we did instead was actually worse. Way worse! We settled. Somehow, we'd become complacent and accepted the "crumbs" life had to offer, with the unspoken assumption it would most likely never change.

Until one day 18 years ago when GOD turned it all around.

It was twelve days before Christmas. Our four kids, then 7 months to 7 years old, didn't realize things were difficult for us, and were all excited about what they were going to get for Christmas. Running around, smiling all the time, giggling, flipping through Toys R' Us catalogs and watching the toy commercials on TV, they were counting the days.

I was jolted awake from my dream, ran to the door, realized there was no pizza delivery guy coming after all. I ran for the phone so I wouldn't miss the call.

It was Chuck calling to tell me that he lost his job.

Great.

Twelve days before Christmas, four kids under seven, already flat broke, bills piled several inches high, furnace ready to give up the ghost any second, and now hubby lost his job.

Just great.

But somehow, as surreal as it seems now, looking back 18 years ago, GOD in HIS amazingly loving way, with HIS overwhelming grace and mercy, caused something to rise up inside me, something I hadn't experienced before: a new sense of courage and hope, and I realized at that second I had an important decision to make.

I had to choose, right there on the spot, how I was going to handle this. It could either be yet another really, really, REALLY bad day, and if so, I'd soon be calling everyone I knew, telling them what happened so they could feel sorry for me. OR I could bite my tongue, take a deep breath, and reassure my husband that all would be OK, and that GOD has a better plan for us anyway.

All the while, in the back of my mind I was reminded of the little "hobby" direct sales business I'd started nine months before. Hmmm… maybe… just maybe…

GOD IS DOING A NEW THING!

Forget the former things; do not dwell on the past. See, I am doing a new thing! Now it springs up, do you not perceive it?

Isaiah 43:18-19b

There was no pizza delivery guy that Wednesday 18 years ago, but what happened when Chuck lost his job was much better.

Although we didn't have pizza that night, we were given the gift of hope. Finally, there was light at the end of a very long, dark tunnel, and the possibility of a bright future.

It was that very day that I decided I would build that little hobby direct sales business into something big. I would figure a way and quitting was not an option. The bridge was burned and there was no going back.

From that day on, we spoke positively about our financial situation, even though it hadn't changed yet. When family and friends called and we explained what happened with Chuck's job, and they naturally replied with worry, we told them that it was actually a very exciting time, and we were going to be OK. (Even though it was the scariest thing we'd ever done up to that point.)

The tide changed that day, with that one decision.

GOD works like that quite often. What seems to be the darkest, most challenging time turns out to be the stepping stone to greater things. GOD knows exactly what HE's doing. HE knows the end of the story, and it's glorious beyond measure.

It reminds me of the unforgettable scene from the Wizard of Oz. Dorothy is in her room, and the whole world is spinning around her, confusing, scary, and chaotic. People and places from her life swirl by her and she's powerless. When the house lands with a huge bang, everything stops spinning, and it's suddenly uncomfortably quiet...

And Dorothy opens the door to a whole new world!

It's breathtaking. She's stunned, mouth wide open and hand to her chest. She can't believe her eyes!

What was formerly dull, black and white and familiar is now colorful and beautiful beyond imagination.

This is Your Decision Time

And right now there stands before you a brand new open door that GOD has prepared just for you.

GOD is about to do a wonderful new thing in your life. HE's going to take you higher; to places and positions and situations you've never even dared to dream of before.

In fact, please put the book down for just a moment wherever you are and say a little prayer. Tell GOD you're ready and willing for the next amazing chapter of your life.

Better yet, if there's any way you can possibly take just a few minutes with your eyes closed to enjoy HIS presence, please do so. Right now. HE's there with you this instant, smiling, waiting, bidding you to come to him. It's between you and HIM.

It's always only been about you and HIM. HE's been with you, right by your side, your entire life. Now HE's calling you to step up higher to where the colors are brighter, the days are more wonderful, the relationships are more amazing, and HIS power is more evident.

HE has hardwired you, before the foundation of the world, with amazing, wonderful, and unique gifts and talents, and HE's calling you forward to use them.

The days of sitting on the sidelines are over!

Now is the appointed time when it all comes together. When GOD will cause you to be a vessel to be used for HIS honor, so that all the world can see HIS glory, YES YOU!

You, the one who was abused. You, the one who's been laughed at. You, the one who's tried different business ventures but failed each time. You, the one with the wayward child. You, the victim of a failed marriage.

HE's been there the whole time, and HE's doing a new thing right now.

Whoever you are, wherever you've been, how dark the darkness you've been through, or how great the success you have had so far... HE's led you here, to this very moment, with this book in your hands.

Days filled with unnecessary worry, fear, stress, and financial troubles can be over quicker than you ever imagined. In fact, you may never have dreamed that you could live a life that was peaceful and that you could literally walk out each and every day with an inexpressible joy, knowing everything is exactly how it should be and that you're going through every motion hand in hand with the most amazing and awesome KING of KINGS!

There before you lays a door and your decision time is now. Are you going to embrace the new, or are you going to hold on to the familiar and comfortable?

Do you believe GOD has something better for you, even though you don't know what it is yet? If so, please make the decision to be OK with the unknown for just a little while with me, I am confident GOD will make things clear to you.

When GOD wants to do a new work, as long as you're willing, NOTHING can stop it. It's up to you. Are you willing to allow HIM to complete the good work that HE's already started in you? If you decide to go for it, really go for it, don't worry: no man can close the door HE has opened wide unto you!

> *See, I have placed before you*
> *an **open door***
> *that no one can shut!*
>
> Revelation 3:8

My prayer for you is that this book is your open door: as you travel with me through the pages of this book, something deep within your soul will be stirred and you'll feel the pull to step out and step up as never before.

We're here to make a difference in the world. These are dark, confusing, and chaotic times we live in; but during times like these, GOD's light shines brighter than ever before. WE ARE THAT LIGHT!

Yes, YOU and me! We ARE the light, and this is a new season we're entering into. The difficulties of yesterday will fade into a distant memory, and all will make sense. We've been prepared for something, and that something is HERE, it's NOW!

Your job is to step into it and receive it. My job is to teach you how!

It's time to chart your course.

It's time to put the difficulties of the past behind you and never look back.

It's time to put aside things that have been holding you back and run with endurance the amazing race set before you.

Don't worry, GOD will guide you, because HE's already got it all planned out.

HE just wants you to start moving.

IT's GAME TIME!

It may be time for you to get that business started, get more involved at church, take on more responsibility at work, stop focusing on yourself and your problems and be a blessing to others, start that blog, take your business or ministry to the next level, break those bad habits, end bad relationships, increase the amount you've been giving, lose weight and get in shape, or whatever you've been wanting to do but haven't started yet.

GOD has a wonderful plan for your life, and it's time to get started, even if you don't know what it is yet. HE will show you. IT'S TIME!

No more excuses.

Exciting right?

Now where the rubber really meets the road is that you need to make "space" for the new by getting rid of the old. And I'm not talking about stuff, I'm talking about old ways of thinking, believing and acting.

No worries, I'll teach you how!

Mary Jo Wehniainen

OUT WITH THE OLD

Most people live their lives on autopilot without even realizing it.

You've been living in your skin 20, 30, 40, 50 years or more, and you're used to yourself and you're comfortable. You do things a certain way, and say certain things without giving it a second thought. It's just how you do things, and you don't stop to consciously ask yourself "Why?"

> A newlywed couple was cooking one of their first meals together. When the bride cut off the ends of the ham before putting it in the pan, her husband asked her why she did that. She told him it was because that's how her mom always did it.
>
> Out of curiosity, the wife asked her mom why she cut off the ends of the ham, and she said it's because that's what her mom always did.
>
> That weekend the wife visited her grandmother and asked why she cut the ends off the ham. The old woman laughed and said, "Oh sweetie, I started that years ago because the ham wouldn't fit in the pan I had!"

This young wife is not alone.

In this case, the only thing lost were the ends of the ham. Unfortunately, there are many things we do unconsciously that do have a negative impact.

You might be hurting yourself and others, struggling with the same frustrations over and over, and don't even realize you're part of the problem! It's normal to assume things are the way they are because of what someone else has done or on your circumstances, but the true source of the problem is oftentimes you!

It's like you're on autopilot. I call it a "default setting."

Your default setting is how you are (or how you act) without even thinking about it. It's almost like a reflex, and is neither good nor bad, unless those tendencies are causing you repeated frustration and trouble. Then it's really bad because it's something you're doing that's hurting you, and oftentimes the people around you, and you have no idea it's going on.

> The way you've always done things is what's gotten you where you are today. If you aren't happy with how things are, you need to change how you do things and what you say!

Many times people have unconsciously created their own default setting so they don't need to step out of their comfort zone.

It might be a single person who'd rather stay home than risk going out and meeting new people and possibly get rejected, so they become sort of a hermit.

Maybe it's someone who botched up a few recipes, and so they've developed the default setting that they don't cook, because they don't want to fail again.

Possibly it's someone in a sales career who's been rejected one too many times and concludes that they're no good at sales, but if they'd just have stayed in the game and refined their skills, they'd be fine.

If you do things a certain way because it's comfortable, you will stay in status-quo for the rest of your life.

That's not what GOD has for you: HE wants you to get uncomfortable!

There are thoughts you've been having and things that you've been doing unconsciously, which you now consciously need to change.

I remember eighteen years ago when I was working very hard on myself; I knew I had a default setting that wasn't set for high levels of success. I decided to shock my system into doing things differently. For a solid week I did everything differently than I would normally do!

> If you're not getting the results you want in your life, you need to change your default setting!

It was really hard, and kind of crazy, but it worked! You might want to try it. (Whether you keep it up for a week or not is up to you!)

It went something like this:

In the morning when I woke up, if I normally brushed my teeth first thing, this particular week I instead went right to the kitchen to make coffee first. If I usually put my pants on with the right leg first, I'd start with the left. If I drove home on a certain route, I'd take another route home. I slept on the other side of the bed.

The real purpose of this crazy exercise was to make me conscious of all the things I do on auto pilot so I could change what wasn't serving me. (No worries, I did go back to brushing my teeth first thing!)

Your default setting consists of three things: what you think, what you say, and what you do.

It comes from a variety of sources, including:
- People you spend time with
- Words that have been said to you
- Comments made by other people
- What you saw or experienced while growing up
- Trauma you've experienced

- Personal rejection (real or perceived)
- The family dynamic you were born into

Here are some examples of things you might hear people saying (or things you might say yourself) that come from a default setting. You hear them all the time, but you may never have realized what they were:

- I never win anything.
- I'm not a very good cook.
- I'm not good at sales.
- I have no time.
- I'm too old.
- You can't teach an old dog new tricks.
- Money doesn't grow on trees.
- I can't afford that.
- I'll never get ahead.
- I'm shy.
- I'm different.
- That might work for her, but it wouldn't work for me.
- Everyone in my family is overweight.

Limiting Beliefs and Invisible Brick Walls

The way you view yourself, the people around you, and the world in general is based on your beliefs and unconscious programming.

The things you do and the way you do them, as well as the words and phrases you say also stem from past programming that may no longer serve you.

Here's a way to figure out what's working and what's not:

The areas in your life where you're successful are most likely where you have good beliefs. In the areas where you're struggling, you

> Limiting beliefs are beliefs that restrain you in some way. They are hard to recognize as they're usually disguised as truth, but they are not the truth. They hold you back from success, happiness, and from reaching your true, GOD-given potential.

most likely have limiting beliefs that do not serve you. This includes relationships, health, finances, etc.

If you never seem to have enough money, you probably have a limiting belief around money. If you're always struggling to keep a job, you likely have a limiting belief around that. If you can't seem to get control of your weight, you have a limiting belief regarding your self-image.

Had I not discovered and corrected a couple of my own limiting beliefs, I would still be the shy, stay-at-home mom who never had enough money, stressed out all the time, and you wouldn't be reading this book right now.

If you've been feeling stuck or frustrated in any way, please pay close attention. The two stories I'm about to share with you were pivotal moments in my life, and may be the key to some of your personal struggles as well. There are likely things that have been running your life in ways you've never considered before.

February of 1997. It was two months after my husband lost his job. Although I was constantly speaking positively about my new business venture, I wasn't having much success. I figured it was because I needed to learn more about how to build a successful direct sales business.

I'd received an invitation in the mail for a three day training event in South Florida and it seemed to be exactly what I needed to learn to make my business successful. The only problem was that we had almost no money left. It would literally cost every last penny we had to buy the ticket to the event, fly me there, and put me in a hotel for three days.

But I was already so far out on a limb regarding my commitment to this business venture, I couldn't turn back now! I felt almost forced to take the financial risk and attend the event.

There were so many wonderful and amazing things that happened those three days, each one a lesson in its own. But the true breakthrough happened the first night, back in my hotel room. The evening ended with a guest speaker who explained that it's often the things we believe that hold us back from true success rather than the mere need to improve our skills. She ended her talk with a challenge for each of us to identify what our limiting belief was.

Back in my hotel room, I had a heart to heart talk with the LORD about my limiting belief, whatever it was. I needed to discover what mine was so I could get over it and get on with success in my business. What HE showed me was the shocker of a lifetime!

My limiting belief was the absolute best ever. It was true! It was so true everyone would agree that I was already doing a great job. They'd empathize with me! But nonetheless, it was a limiting belief that I not only believed, but I realized I said quite often in regards to my business, and it was the very thing holding me back from success.

"I do all I can do with five kids."

That was my limiting belief!

Come on, it was true. Give me a little credit: I had five kids under eight years old. I homeschooled. Two were in diapers and the others needed constant supervision. I led a natural food co-op, and now I was starting a business. To say "I do all I can do with five kids" was really an understatement...

But it was crystal clear to me that those exact words were the very thing that had been holding me back. It was the limiting belief I unconsciously hid behind.

If "I do all I can do with five kids" was true, than there was no reason for me to try harder or learn more, because I already put that disclaimer on my efforts and results.

> The thing that is holding you back is not real!

The second I uncovered the limiting belief that was holding me back, it all immediately changed. It's not that I suddenly knew what to do differently, and my business didn't magically grow to six-figures overnight, but I knew that the thing that was holding me back was not real.

It was just a belief that I'd unconsciously been hiding behind! GOD opened my eyes to the truth...

And two years later, I was named one of the top 20 business builders out of half a million people in that company!

My second limiting belief was much more insidious than the first. In fact, it wasn't just a limiting belief, this one was a monstrous, invisible brick wall!

It was something right in front of me that was HUGE, and blocked me at every turn, but I had no idea what it was!

Even after I was having great success in my direct sales business, I still had this nagging feeling that somehow I was different from the folks who were "ultra-successful." You know, the top income earners, the ones they tell stories about. It was as if they were in another group of people altogether, and I somehow wasn't part of that group.

It's really hard to describe, sort of a sense that pervaded me deep down within my core, which caused me to believe that even though I was working hard, and had commendable levels of success, I was somehow different than "those" people. They were the really successful ones, and I was just a faker. They were different, in some intangible way I couldn't put my finger on, and it bugged the heck out of me.

I knew that whatever this "invisible" thing was, it was the thing that was keeping me from the higher levels of success that I desired. I was never going to be part of that "group" of people no matter how hard I tried unless I uncovered it.

So I spent time asking the LORD about it. A LOT of time, because I needed to break free from whatever was holding me back.

And then one day it hit me like a ton of bricks!

It was something I'd grown up hearing from my mom and it was quite innocent. She never intended any harm, and had she known that all these years later it would be a topic in a book, I'm sure she would have changed her words immediately.

This is what I'd hear my mom say all the time as she described relatives, co-workers, friends and neighbors:

"Oh, well they have money".

"Must be nice to have money like them."

"Oh, yeah, things are easy for them, because they have money."

As if "they" were part of an entirely different group of people than our family!

She repeated these innocent statements all the time! I felt I belonged to a group who didn't have money.

I'd been brainwashed as a child by an innocent phrase and it held me back my whole life. I could finally see the truth.

There really wasn't anything different between me and "those" people after all! It was an illusion, a perception, that was ingrained in me since childhood.

And once I saw it, and realized it wasn't true, things immediately changed from deep within.

Just like when I discovered my limiting belief was "I do all I can do with five kids" everything immediately changed!

And ten years and several businesses later, I was the person earning more in one hour than I formerly earned in a entire month! Crazy, I know!

I guarantee this would never have happened had I not identified the "invisible brick wall" that had been keeping me stuck in status quo.

So what is it for you?

Do you ever get the sense that there's something holding you back? Something you deal with repeatedly that keeps causing you problems and stress?

It may come from what you saw, heard and experienced growing up; what people have said to you throughout the years; excuses you made up yourself (unconsciously) and then started believing; traumas you've faced; news reports, etc.

What were some of the things you heard while growing up that have become stumbling blocks and invisible brick walls for you?

There are lots of them concerning money, I wonder if any of these may have affected you?
- Money doesn't grow on trees
- We can't afford that
- No you can't have that
- Money is tight
- Must be nice to have money
- Money is the root of all evil

According to the Bible, it's the "love" of money that's the root of all evil, not the money itself! (1 Timothy 6:10)

You will most likely have to ponder this awhile because it is something you're so accustomed to you don't even see it. In fact, you may need someone else to help you recognize it.

I'm now so tuned in to these sort of things that I can often hear them immediately in a conversation I have with someone. They don't even realize anything is wrong, but I already know what it is by the very words they say to me.

This happened to me just a few weeks ago with someone I'm in contact with on a regular basis.

Every time I speak with her the topic of money being tight always comes up. Every single time! It comes up about the cost of her kid's education, the amount of money she and her husband earn, how expensive everything is these days, and on and on.

Then one day when we were talking, she mentioned something about how her parents raised her, and how her husband's parents raised him. So, my curiosity was up because I know this came from somewhere and is a huge brick wall for her, even though she thinks it's her reality.

It turns out that both she and her husband had to work really hard for everything they had from an early age because both sets of parents had always expressed that they never had enough money! Voila! That was it. As young children, she and her husband had to earn their own money for clothes, going out, and the extra things all kids enjoy but aren't a necessity.

> If you are frustrated in any area of your life, you are likely being run by your default setting.

(It may not have had anything to do with how much money either set of parents actually had, it had to do with their beliefs that they passed down to the kids: my friend and her husband!)

Unfortunately, my friend will most likely always struggle with money, no matter how much she has, until she realizes the invisible brick wall she's been up against, and where it came from.

If you are frustrated in any area of your life, there are likely things that have been impacting you that you're not aware of. It's time to be free once and for all!

And if you happen to think that you're too far gone, or that the things that have happened to you are too bad and you'll never experience true freedom, there could be nothing further from the truth!

Those exact thoughts and statements are your limiting beliefs, and your invisible brick walls.

- If anyone ever finds out the truth about my past they

won't like me!
- Nobody in my family has ever been successful.
- I'll never be able to afford a home like that.
- Some people get all the breaks.
- I'm too busy to start a business.
- I can't save money because I can barely make ends meet.

GOD will Use Your Difficulties for HIS Glory

And we know that in all things GOD works for the good of those who love HIM, who have been called according to HIS purpose.

Romans 8:28

Once you realize you've been living your life unconsciously, you can start making conscious choices about what you do from here on out.

The difficulties you've experienced in your life will become your advantages; it's during the challenging times of life that we grow. Had my husband not lost his job 18 years ago, I hate to even imagine what my life might be like now!

Here are some examples from the Bible:

Had Joseph not been thrown in prison for a crime he didn't commit, an entire nation could have perished due to severe famine. (Genesis 29)

Had Abraham and Sarah been able to conceive a child easily, there wouldn't have been such an amazing story about GOD's faithfulness, and what it means to believe GOD's promises are true. (Genesis 17 & 21)

Had Ruth lived a "happily-ever-after-life" with her first

husband, she would never have connected with Boaz, and JESUS was eventually born into that genealogy! (The book of Ruth)

GOD has everything under control, and HE knows exactly what HE's doing!

Overcoming challenges and setbacks is how we grow. It's part of life, and part of GOD's plan for us. If everything was easy we wouldn't be strong in spirit, we'd be weak!

When GOD tests us through challenging times, HE's actually making us stronger!

> *I will refine them like silver and test them like gold. They will call on MY Name and I will answer them; I will say "They are MY people," and they will say "The LORD is our GOD!"*
>
> Zechariah 13:9

With GOD, nothing that happens escapes HIS attention, and HE will turn it all around and use it for HIS glory!

It's time to set aside the old way of being (and believing) and embrace the wonderful, new, amazing, powerful life GOD has for you!

> *Therefore, if anyone is in Christ, he is a new creation; old things have passed away; behold, all things have become new.*
>
> *2 Corinthians 5:17*

What are your limiting beliefs?

What do you keep saying to yourself that's holding you back?

What excuses are you giving for why you can't do more and have more in your life?

What will you start saying instead?

What do you remember hearing as a child that has held you back?

If you're having any sort of financial difficulties, there's a good chance it stems from your past.

What was said about money and people who had money when you were growing up?

What are some of the major obstacles and challenges that you've faced in your life? (The things GOD WILL turn around for HIS glory!).

Mary Jo Wehniainen

NEXT-LEVEL CHRISTIANITY™

Next-Level Christians™ are people who aren't afraid to step out and trust the LORD, even though they don't know exactly where HE's leading them. They prove themselves faithful by using the gifts and talents the LORD has given them, and then the LORD promotes them. They put other people first. They're the ones who dare to do what others won't even try, the ones starting businesses, funding ministries, stepping into the spotlight, running for office, writing books, meeting the needs of their community. They are the most approachable, most relatable, most genuine people on the planet... filled with HIS wisdom, HIS peace, HIS love and HIS grace! No matter what line of work they're in, they're in high demand and constantly being honored.

So there I was, 18 years ago, a shy, stay-at-home mom, flat broke and stressed to the max, and my hubby just lost his job. I knew it was a pivotal time, and I had to take stock of what I had to work with. That's how GOD always starts too!

GOD always starts right where you're at, with what you already have on hand to work with!

David's amazing story in 1 Samuel 17 began when he heard Goliath defy the armies of the Living GOD, and he immediately took action. He was a young man of great courage and knew GOD so intimately that he was sure GOD would be with him. King Saul tried to prepare David by dressing him in his personal coat of armor and bronze helmet, but David couldn't wear these because they were not the tools GOD provided for him.

Instead he grabbed his sling and five smooth stones, and fearlessly approached the giant... and the rest is history. Little did anyone dare to imagine that David could take down the huge giant with a single stone!

Think about the boy with five loaves and two fish in John 6:5-15. Jesus took what he had and five thousand men were fed, besides women and children... and there were twelve basketfuls of broken pieces left over! The disciples could never have dreamed that this small contribution, along with GOD's mighty power, could feed this multitude.

2 Kings 4 tells the story of a widow who was about to have her two boys taken from her as payment because she couldn't pay her debt. The Old Testament prophet Elisha asked her what she had to work with, to which she replied, "Nothing at all except a little oil."

A little oil? How in the world could that help her keep her boys and pay her creditor?

Elisha instructed her to go around and ask all her neighbors for empty jars, and not to ask for just a few. Once she had gotten the jars, she began pouring the oil into the jars and it didn't run out until all the jars were full. She then sold the oil, paid off her debts, and was able to keep her sons and live off the remaining proceeds.

Side note: the size of the blessing she received was directly equal to the number of jars she gathered. This is very important, and I will teach you more about this a little later in Chapter 5: The U.P.L.I.F.T. Formula™ to Success with GOD.

◇◇◇◇◇◇

John 21 starts out with the disciples fishing through the night, disappointed because they didn't catch anything. When Jesus came on the scene and told them to throw the net on the right side of the boat, they did, and they were unable to haul the net in because of the huge number of fish!

Now these were expert fisherman, and they'd been working hard all night to no avail. But in obedience to the LORD, they used what they'd been given (even though they were probably thinking "we've tried that and it didn't work.") BUT the number of fish was so great they couldn't even handle it!

◇◇◇◇◇◇

Do you see a common thread? GOD always works through what HE's already given you to work with! Even if you've tried and failed many times, and even if it's something very small!

The bottom line is that you have everything you need, right now, to get started towards the miraculous life that GOD wants you to have!

> You already have everything you need to get started toward the miraculous life GOD wants you to have!

When you use what you already have at hand, and step out with the LORD, the most amazing things will happen! Once you're in motion, GOD will start directing you and changing course with you. The important thing is that you get started.

Next-Level Christians™ are people who aren't afraid to take that step with the LORD, even though they don't have the entire plan laid out before them.

You have to prove yourself faithful with what HE's already given you to work with and HE will give you more responsibility, and greater success. That could be at your job, at home, with your finances, in your health, how you deal with others, etc.

For me, what I had to work with at that time was a teeny tiny direct sales business I'd started about nine months prior to the day my husband lost his job. It was just a hobby. In fact, when I started the business my goal was to earn $300 a month. My thinking was so small at that time that I actually believed an extra $300 a month would change my life.

Little did I know GOD had a way bigger plan!

Even though I had no idea how to build a direct sales business, I knew other people were having great success, and I believed GOD could help me too.

What I instinctively knew from the moment Chuck lost his job was that I needed to take my business seriously. It was no longer a hobby. It was the thing GOD was going to use to provide for our family.

I worked on it every single day. I called everyone I knew, even though I hadn't talked to many of those people for 10 or more years, and had no idea what I should be saying or how to give a good presentation. I didn't let my lack of knowledge or my fear stop me.

It was really all about stepping out, being courageous and determined, and keep "showing up" even when those around me started wimping out and whining, or telling me all the reasons I wouldn't succeed.

I didn't get off to the fastest start, but I made progress nonetheless. It was a busy, exciting time! While I worked on my new business, I also worked very hard on myself. I listened to dozens of audio training programs, took classes and enrolled in coaching programs to improve my skills.

In fact, the only peaceful time I had to think was when I was in the shower. GOD would always put someone on my heart and as soon as I came out, I'd call them. That was my crazy business-building method at that time. My telephone conversations were long and drawn out, not very effective, and most days I ran out the charge on several phones as I was going from room to room running away from kids! But I was making progress.

It's pretty funny when I think about it. One of the funniest memories my kids have about that time is my habit of blasting a motivational cassette tape in the bathroom while I was showering, every single day. They could hear it through the door: "YOU CAN DO IT, YOU KNOW YOU CAN. YOU WERE MEANT TO DO IT. PEOPLE LIKE YOU. THEY WANT TO TALK TO YOU. YOU WILL SUCCEED."

Too funny, right? But it worked!

I also remember the eight foot long kid height oak wood table in the "homeschool" room in our house. The seats were about 12" off the ground, just the right size for a four-year old, but way too small for a grown woman, especially when I was pregnant with Grace. Nevertheless, this was the place where I sat every single night to make my calls. I'd have my script written out, and the list of people to call. And I'd call.

When I ran out of people to call, I started going out in the attempt of meeting new people to talk to. At first I was shy, but I knew if I didn't step out of my comfort zone and find some people to talk to, I'd never succeed. I also joined the gym, a toastmasters group, and attended a lot of business networking events.

Even though it was scary, and I never did anything like this before, I kept working at it and using what I had, just like David and his stones. And I knew GOD was smiling down on me.

I would host small gatherings at my home once a week. It was a huge challenge getting the house cleaned and the kids fed and put to bed before the meeting started. I remember a few times waiting in the recliner for my guests to come, and I fell asleep in the chair, only to wake up several hours later to the truth that no one came after all. Rejections from my guests couldn't stop me; I was working with what GOD had given me.

Several years later, one of my friends who'd been at my very first home meeting confessed that as he sat there, he looked at me the entire time, feeling so sorry for me, because he knew I'd never be a success.

I also remember when I was big, fat, and pregnant with baby Grace, driving several hours to an event by myself, because no one else would come.

I just kept doing it and doing it and doing it, with GOD as my business partner. Slowly and surely, my business grew.

March 1999, twenty-seven months after the time my husband lost his job, I was at the big annual company convention in Dallas, TX with a group of my teammates. There were over 10,000 people in attendance, and it was an amazing time. It was the last evening of the event, and we were sitting in one of the very back rows, way up at the top of the stadium. We enjoyed hearing all the success stories and the trainings. And then they came to the part of the program where they gave out awards for various achievements. They began calling out the names of the top 20 business builders of that year, and they called my name! I couldn't believe it, and thought I heard it wrong, but all of my friends were looking at me, jumping up and down and clapping. I was speechless! As the tears rolled down my cheeks, with my mouth wide open I somehow managed to make my way down through the crowd, to the stage, and received my award.

> When you step out in faith with GOD at your side, HE will not let you down!

It was so amazing! All because I made a decision, trusted GOD, worked hard, and never turned back.

GOD took me from being a shy, stay-at-home mom with a teeny tiny home-based business and a goal of earning $300 a month, to one of the top 20 business builders out of ½ a million people in that company!

So my question for you is: What do you have to work with? What has GOD already given you that you haven't yet put to

good use?
- Do you love to serve others?
- Are you creative?
- Do you love animals?
- Do you love to write?
- Are you great with technical things?
- Are you a natural-born salesperson?
- Do you love to cook?

Whatever it is that you have to work with, ask the LORD to show you ways you can begin "stepping" into that immediately!

If you love to cook, start inviting people over to your home for dinner, enroll in culinary school, volunteer to make meals for people at your church.

If you're a natural born salesperson, start selling something!

If you love to write, you can start your own blog on a topic that interests you.

You get the idea!

And GOD already has the plan set out for you. You just need to get moving!

It's time to set foot into the Jordan

You may be familiar with the amazing story of Joshua leading the Israelites into the Promised Land. They needed to cross the flooded Jordan River. The LORD told Joshua to have the priests stand in the Jordan and when they did so the waters would stop flowing and stand up in a heap. The priests obeyed, took the first step into flood-level waters, and the river literally stood up in a heap so the Israelites could cross through on dry ground. It defied everything that was possible! (Joshua 3)

It's the same with us today. We need to step out in faith, knowing that GOD has our back, and once we step out HE can start moving us around as HE wants. That's when things get really exciting!

But if we don't take the first step, nothing will happen!

We have to be willing to move even though we don't know the

entire plan. In fact, GOD almost never shows you the entire plan before you take that first step. So if that's what you've been waiting for, you may as well forget it. That's what having faith is all about!

I pretty much live my life with both feet in the Jordan, and every day I'm stepping out and doing things that the LORD directs me to do.

I'm about to share four of the bigger "steps" I've taken over the years.

Had I been afraid and backed down from any one of these, I hate to think about what I would have missed out on. Each of these steps of faith has led to tremendous growth in the LORD and then another step. That's just how GOD works!

Several years before I was married, I became born-again and was part of a wonderful church and amazing group of friends who really loved the LORD. My life was so exciting, and I had no desire to change anything.

One evening, I had a dream I was sitting across the desk from a gentleman I was working for, but I didn't recognize him. It was a brief dream, but when I woke up I knew for sure it was very significant, and a dream that the LORD had given me.

I didn't take any action on it, because there was no apparent action to take! I just vividly remembered the man I was working for, even though I had no idea who he was.

About that same time, out church was hosting a community event where we read through the entire Bible out loud, cover to cover, in our town square.

All the church members took turns filling hour long shifts, 24 hours a day. It was in conjunction with a special project by the Christian Broadcasting Network (CBN) out of Virginia Beach. They had just released a special version of the Bible called The Book, and that was the version we were reading from.

The folks at The 700 Club decided to send a film crew down to our community to do a TV piece featuring our church's project. I'd never watched the show prior to that time because there was no cable TV where I lived, but I did watch it at a friend's home knowing they were going to be filming us.

My jaw dropped when I first saw Pat Robertson, CBN Founder and 700 Club host on TV. He was the man in my dream!

While the film crew was with us, I spoke with one of the cameramen and told him about my dream. He graciously offered to let me stay with him and his wife should I decide to come to Virginia Beach to explore the possibilities of working at CBN.

Wow! Being a new Christian, this was pretty exciting. I wasn't accustomed to the LORD's way of putting things together like this.

The following week I called the HR department of CBN and thankfully connected with a lovely woman who was very sensitive to the HOLY SPIRIT, and although my phone call could have seemed strange, she took it seriously and explained the procedure for applying for a job at CBN.

I went through all the red tape, including numerous interviews, and eventually ended up being hired as one of the assistants in Pat Robertson's office.

I left my family and friends in Florida and moved to Virginia Beach. It was wonderful and amazing, but a huge step into the unknown and scary at the same time.

It was there that I met my husband Chuck, and we settled and raised our five kids.

(What if I hadn't taken that step?)

The next pivotal big step is the story I already shared with you when Chuck lost his job, and I got serious about my little hobby direct sales business. Although, I never did anything like that before, I knew it was the LORD leading me into uncharted territory. Again, HE did not disappoint. GOD caused me to prosper beyond anything I ever dreamed possible and I became one of the top 20 business builders out of half a million people, and our family lived quite an enviable life. Not only were we able to go grocery shopping and buy whatever we wanted, we also were able to take months off at a time for family fun!

Of course, there were many other wonderful GOD stories in between, too numerous to share, but the next really big one happened in 2006.

Our family moved to South Florida two years prior, in 2004, when I accepted the position of partner in a direct sales training company. My entire family had always wanted to move to Florida, and I was a coach and trainer in the direct sales industry already, so it seemed like the perfect fit.

During my time there, the company had great success and grew tremendously; and so did my responsibilities. I went from having my own business where I was free to come and go as I pleased, and could even go away with my family for months at a time, to being cooped up in an office at least 8 hours a day, and then came home to teach classes on the phone at night.

The money I earned was great -- but I no longer had time with my family, and that wasn't good at all.

The LORD made it very clear to me that my time at the company was coming to an end. My challenge was that I was earning close to $200K a year with that company, and my family was heavily dependent on the income because we had a high overhead.

I knew the LORD wanted me to leave, but didn't know where HE was leading me, and because I held such a busy and demanding role at that company, I was unable to set up another job before I made the move.

So, I again put my foot in the Jordan, which felt much more like jumping off a cliff in a freefall. I had to mentally and emotionally prepare myself to make a move of that magnitude, so I spent a lot of time with the LORD in prayer and reading the WORD and other motivational books that helped me believe I could do it. Finally I had the peace I needed to move forward. I knew HE would take care of me!

I gave notice that I would be leaving, but we didn't set up a definite end date because I had so much work to do to get others ready to handle the various roles I'd been responsible for. After about six weeks of training the folks who were going to take over my responsibilities, I was told I was no longer needed, and that very day was my last day. Talk about sudden and scary!

That Sunday I waited around after church so I could have a quick word with my pastor. I gave him a check made out to the church for 10 percent of my severance pay, and explained the situation, and asked him to pray for me. He was a little cautious about the move I made, and told me to make sure I wasn't doing anything foolish. I just smiled because I knew GOD had my back even though it was definitely one of the bravest, boldest things I'd ever done up to that point.

The next thing I did was to put up a really simple website in which I offered a free class for people in direct sales businesses. It had a simple headline, my picture, an audio message that played when they went to the site, and a sign up form on the page so they could register for the class. I had email addresses for about 90 people I'd met over the previous several years, and I invited them to the free class. Some of those folks shared the invitation with their friends, and over 1,000 people attended my first free teleconference training.

At the end of the class I offered a five-week group coaching class where I would teach them in greater detail the secrets and skills I'd perfected over the years, and over 100 people enrolled in that class!

Within two weeks of leaving my position, I'd earned over $30,000.

The LORD showed me exactly what to do, and I obeyed. It was truly amazing!

In fact, the money came in so fast that PayPal shut me down temporarily until they could verify that I wasn't doing anything illegal for so much money to come in so quickly on a brand new account.

That was the beginning of my coaching practice, and over the next several years I was blessed with the privilege of training thousands of people around the world to have greater success in their businesses.

And the most exciting to date, is where we are today, at the very beginning of Success With GOD International. GOD has been preparing me for this work my entire life. It is a HUGE step of faith in many ways, and I believe millions of lives will be forever changed, once again, just because I said YES to GOD. Already the miracles HE's bringing to pass each and every day take my breath away, and are far too numerous to count.

Again, these are just a handful of many steps of faith I've taken over the years.

In between big steps up, there's often a "holding place" or plateau, which can be a difficult place to be if you don't understand what's going on. That's why it's so important to see things from GOD's perspective.

These times of "waiting" or "standing still" is when GOD tests us to see what's really in our heart, and makes sure HE can trust us with even more responsibility. Just like Joseph had to spend 13 years as an Egyptian slave and then in prison before becoming second in command of all Egypt. (Genesis 37-41)

Once you step out in faith is when GOD can work with you. That's when HE will start maneuvering you into the places HE wants you to go. But if you don't take the first step, HE's not going to drag you!

So, where is GOD leading you to step into the Jordan? You may already have a pretty good idea. The best place to start is to think about what you already have to work with.

Be Flexible and Wholehearted

GOD is constantly leading you, and it's very important that you remain flexible in HIS hand. Sometimes things may not make sense at first, but I assure you HE is in control. HE wants you to completely trust HIM, to really understand and believe that HE has your back. So, even though you believe you may know fully what HIS upcoming plan is for you, don't be surprised as it takes twists and turns. It's just how HE rolls!

> *Serve wholeheartedly, as if you were serving the LORD...*
>
> *Ephesians 6:7*

But while HE's leading you along, it's very important that everything you do is done wholeheartedly.

Whether you're an employee at a job you love or a job you're not too fond of, work wholeheartedly as unto the LORD.

You may be going to school or a stay-at-home mom. Whatever GOD has called you to do, do it wholeheartedly with a spirit of excellence.

Next-Level Christians™ should be the ones everyone's begging to hire because of your reputation and spirit of excellence.

You are more powerful than you think!

GOD has put tremendous creative power in your hands, even though you may have never tapped into it

> When you're in step and in tune with GOD, HIS plan becomes your plan. HIS vision becomes your vision. HIS will becomes your will.

before. And the power HE's put inside you has everything to do with what your future will look like. It's up to you to receive it!

Your life is truly a blank canvas. Whatever's happened in the past is the past. The future is up to you, with GOD as your partner.

HE wants you to have an amazing life, a life that is so

awesome that people want to meet your GOD!

Remember, Next-Level Christians™ are the ones who dare to do what others won't even try. They're the ones starting the businesses, funding the ministries, stepping into the spotlight, running for office, writing the books, meeting the needs of their community, and more.

If you're reading this book, there's a good change you have a sense that GOD has something more for you.

Are you ready to step out and become a Next-Level Christian™?

THE U.P.L.I.F.T. FORMULA™ TO SUCCESS WITH GOD

When I began coaching people over twelve years ago, I sat down to really think about what GOD taught me to do that took me from being a shy, stay-at-home mom, always stressed out and broke, to earning more in one hour than most people earn in an entire month!

I discovered there were specific things HE taught me to do, that I've been doing now for the past 18 years, and this formula is at the core of everything I teach.

It's called the U.P.L.I.F.T. Formula™ to Success With God.

This Formula, like any good recipe, requires that all the ingredients are included. You cannot leave anything out! If you want to fully experience all the wonderful things GOD has planned for you, you must implement all these steps.

I have worked with people in the past who've implemented all the steps and their lives were completely transformed, and others who've tried to skip one or two, and they didn't get the results they'd hoped for.

When you apply these principles, and get better and better every day, GOD will show up in a HUGE way in your life. In fact, you may not even recognize yourself in the near future.

There are six steps to the U.P.L.I.F.T. Formula™ to Success With GOD. I go into each of the steps in detail but I wanted you to be able to see them all here:

Unplug From the Negative

Plug In to GOD

Listen Intently

Immediately Obey

Find Your Gift and Focus

Talk, Trust and Tune In to Miracles!

Unplug From the Negative

The first step is to stop putting negative stuff into your mind, your heart and your emotions…

I was driving down the highway a couple months ago, when a phone call came in from one of the people I was coaching at the time. I didn't take the call when it first came in, but listened to the voicemail and immediately called him back because he sounded badly shaken.

He explained how the day before he literally thought he was going to have a heart attack and die. He was beside himself, making sure his wife knew how to access their different financial accounts in the event he did die, because he'd been the one handling their finances up to that point.

As I listened to him, I could tell he was still in crisis mode. It was surprising because just two days before he was absolutely fine. I prayed for him while I was driving, and we set up a time to meet in person later that evening.

We got together, and I asked him to tell me what was going on. It quickly became crystal clear that he had been riddled with fear, and that's why he thought he was going to have a heart attack. The stress he was under was almost too much for him to bear.

Through a series of questions, I discovered that right before bed he'd been watching the financial reports, stock market, etc., on TV because he had a lot of money invested at that time.

That was it! Pure and simple! When I asked him more about this, he quickly saw it too. He was putting huge doses of stress, fear and worry into himself right before he went to bed, and it almost literally cost him his life!

He had the biggest ah-ha moment ever. I literally saw the weight of the world come off his shoulders as we were together that evening, and when I saw him again the next day, he looked like a new man.

Do not underestimate the influence negative news and negative input of all sorts has on you. In fact, if I taught you nothing else, and if you merely eliminated the negative input in your life, you would definitely see a dramatic improvement in the level of peace you experience.

> **The Top 10 Most Common Negative Influences**
> - Certain people
> - TV shows (particularly news programs)
> - Radio shows (again, especially news programs)
> - Your surroundings
> - Bad habits (that make you feel guilty)
> - Repeated conversations that go nowhere
> - Other people's emotions
> - Sad stories
> - Songs with negative lyrics
> - Movies, especially on the big screen (particularly those with a strong emotional pull: fear, violence, sadness, etc.)

At the time of the writing of this book, the news stations are filled with reports of Flight 370 that went missing en route from Kuala Lumpur to Beijing. It's very sad, and still quite a mystery, with all sorts of speculation about what happened.

My son Daniel fell asleep last evening with the TV on, and when I woke up the next morning, the news was giving brief profiles of some of the passengers on the plane.

Ever since I heard about this disaster, I've been praying for those folks and their families and loved ones. I care about every individual and want peace for each of them but, at the same time, I've learned to be careful not to get caught up in other people's emotions.

We always need to be watchful over this.

It might be that you wake up one morning happy and energetic, optimistic that it's going to be a great day, but by the time you get to your office, your enthusiasm is gone and you don't know why.

What happened? Chances are you had something negative come into your psyche, without even realizing it.

If you had the TV on in the morning, even if you were watching a harmless, happy show, the commercials are horrible! Drugs with side effects, legal advertisements talking about why you should sue someone, trailers for scary or violent upcoming movies and shows…

Or maybe you had the radio on as you drove to work. Of course, news reports will definitely get you down, but even a good show has advertisements that play on your emotions. Again, all without you even realizing what's going on!

Or maybe you had a phone call or received a negative text message…

Or perhaps you passed an accident or drove in traffic where everyone around you was pretty agitated…

Pay attention to these things and do the very best you can to eliminate as many negative influences as possible.

Plug In to GOD

So now that you see the importance of unplugging yourself from the many negative influences in your life, you need to get yourself "plugged in" to the right things.

The primary thing you need to plug into, by far, is GOD and HIS WORD!

The WORD of GOD is literally our food! We need it daily to grow and become the person GOD intends us to be!

It is written, "Man shall not live on bread alone but on every word that comes from the mouth of GOD."

Matthew 4:4

What I'm about to share with you is the one most pivotal thing that has dramatically changed my life forever, without a doubt!

I've been born again for over 30 years, and have loved the LORD passionately all that time. I have never been a wishy-washy Christian, and have always loved the WORD of GOD, but somehow I never quite made it a daily discipline, until about six years ago.

It was a challenging time of my life and I somehow got my hands on a devotional 1-year Bible study guide that was exactly what I needed. Funny how GOD always provides exactly what we need at just the right time!

The study was broken up into weeks. The first day of the week you'd read certain parts of a particular book of the Bible, then the other six days you'd answer questions about the story, the people, GOD's role in all of it, think about how you would feel if you were one of the people involved, etc.

I started reading through it, and couldn't put it down. It wasn't that the study itself was so profound, it was that I finally, after all those many years, developed such a hunger and eagerness to consume the WORD that I just couldn't get enough. It was as if it truly had become my daily nourishment that I couldn't live without.

And then GOD led me to do something else that I've been doing now daily for over six years. Writing the WORD!

So, if you were to come to my house today, I could show you hundreds of spiral bound journals that I've written in over the past six years, all full of the WORD!

Keep in mind, what I write are not my words, or my thoughts about things... I write GOD's WORD!

And since I've been doing this now for over six years, I've come across many studies that prove when you write something, versus just reading or hearing, it becomes deeply embedded into your conscious and subconscious mind.

It's truly amazing! By writing the WORD, things pop out at you that you don't see when you're just reading it. You also end up memorizing scripture without even trying!

And so every day for over six years now, I wake up very early in the morning, usually around 4 am before the rest of my family gets up. I make a cup of coffee, go to my favorite chair with my Bible, my journal and a pack of colored pens in hand, and start reading the WORD. I don't write everything I read, but I do write any passages that jump out at me.

I'll write them, I'll underline them, I'll put a box around them. And I may write them again.

I especially like doing this early in the morning when I'm much more receptive than I would be at other times of the day.

This is by far the most important time of my day, each and every day, and I never miss my date with the LORD.

In fact, it's become such a strong habit that I can't wait to go to bed at night because I look so forward to my time with GOD in the morning.

When I talk about this, people always ask me what I read each day, and wonder what sort of Bible reading plan I use. I don't! In fact, I often read and write the same things over and over and over again! Many times GOD leads me to what HE wants me to read, and it's always amazingly on target with what I specifically need for that day.

If you were to look through those hundreds of spiral notebooks, you'd see that there are specific scriptures that I focused on during certain times of my life, depending on things I was going through.

The more deeply we meditate on the WORD, especially the same scriptures over and over, the deeper they go, and the depth of our wisdom and understanding from this practice is magnified many times over!

It really doesn't matter what you read. Start with a Bible reading plan if you like, or start with some favorite scriptures, or some favorite books of the Bible. I definitely have favorites, a lot of them in the Old Testament. I LOVE the book of Isaiah, especially the later chapters, of course Psalms and Proverbs, Joshua, Deuteronomy, Ruth and Esther, just to name a few.

If you're new to the Bible, I'd suggest starting with the Gospel of John, and then maybe also a chapter in Proverbs each day. There are 31 chapters, so you can coordinate them with the date you're reading.

Some of the wonderful side effects of immersing yourself in the WORD like this on a daily basis are:
- you know what GOD is thinking.
- you hear HIM speak to you.
- you have great peace in the midst of turmoil around you.
- you know for sure GOD wants you to succeed.
- you love people.
- you encourage others without trying.
- you see miracles happen around you all day long.
- you have no fear of bad news, financial worries, etc.
- you know GOD has your back.
- your mind is focused on HIS WORD and HIS promises all day long.
- you're happy and peaceful most of the time!

But his DELIGHT is in the law of the LORD, and in HIS law he meditates day and night. He will be like a tree planted by the rivers of water, which yields fruit in its season... Whatever he does prospers!

Psalm 1:2-3

Listen Intently

One of the most wonderful things about walking with the LORD is that HE is always there. Every second of every day, and HE's always got something to say, you just need to listen!

HE speaks as if you're in a conversation with HIM, and you are!

And that's what HE wants.

HE didn't create you so that you go on living a life on your own, HE created you so that you have constant fellowship with HIM!

HE's your father, your coach, your doctor, your lawyer, your Savior, HE bought you with a very great price, and HE wants to be in constant communion with you. You just need to learn to listen!

Whether you turn to the right or to the left, your ears will hear a voice behind you, saying, "This is the way; walk in it."

Isaiah 30:21

When you read the Bible, and all the stories about Joshua, David, Joseph, and more, take note of how many times the Bible states "the LORD said" or "the LORD spoke to" even when the LORD was not physically present.

I'd love to see a Bible that has these words highlighted in some special way, because it's full of them! And the more you take notice of this, the more you'll see throughout history how GOD spoke to HIS children, and the more you can understand how HE still speaks today!

> *Speak, LORD, for your servant is listening.*
>
> 1 Samuel 3:9

One of the reasons reading and writing the WORD is so awesome is that it forces you to see things you may not have seen before. How many times you've read "the LORD said" and it went unnoticed, but when you read the words "the LORD said" in a very receptive, uninterrupted state, and even write those words, it's powerful!

In fact, GOD speaks to us more now than in all the great stories in the Bible that occurred before JESUS ascended into Heaven, because HIS HOLY SPIRIT lives in us! It's as if the HOLY SPIRIT is hovering over the Earth, always there, always speaking, always guiding.

> *Listen, listen to ME and eat what is good, And your soul will delight in the richest of fare.*
>
> Isaiah 55:2

HE wouldn't say listen unless we could hear.

HE hasn't stopped talking, not at all!

It's just that we live in such a noisy, busy world, that it takes a bit of effort to get tuned in enough so you can listen. Once you do, and you stay in constant, daily communication with HIM, listening TAKES NO EFFORT AT ALL!

The closest thing I can compare HIS still small voice to is kind of like when you pay attention to your conscience. Maybe you're going to do something you shouldn't do, and something inside you says "don't." HIS voice is kind of like that.

We have HIS SPIRIT living inside us, so it only makes sense!

> *MY sheep listen to MY voice;*
> *I know them, and they follow ME.*
>
> *John 10:27*

Don't Act Weird!

Now even though I'm telling you that GOD wants to talk to you all day long, PLEASE don't take this as a license to act weird. The worst thing in the world are Christians who give GOD a black-eye, so to speak, because they act strange.

Our two-way relationship with the LORD should be as natural as breathing. It shouldn't be at all obvious to the people around us, and 99.999% of the time that HE speaks to us personally, it's NOT so that we can turn around and tell someone else "The LORD just said…" That would be weird!

No, HE wants us to be the most approachable, the most relatable, the most genuine people on the planet, filled with HIS wisdom, HIS peace, HIS love and HIS grace!

We listen to HIM so we know what to do, how to act, what to say, where to go; NOT so we can go around telling people that we're talking to GOD!

PLEASE, and this bears repeating, Christians should be the most peaceful, loving, happy, "together" people on the face of the earth! We should be the farthest thing from "weird" as can be.

Just think about JESUS's ministry when HE walked on the earth. HE went to the people that the "church" didn't normally go to. HE related to those people and made them feel loved and welcomed. HE was so approachable that HIS personality was magnetic to people. That's how you should be as a believer.

In order to hear HIS voice, you need to spend daily time in HIS WORD, so you get to know HIS heart and HIS character.

If you try to listen but you're not spending time in the WORD, you most likely will be confused, and you will not hear HIS voice clearly. In fact, you may think you are hearing HIS voice, but it may not be. What you're tuning into are your own thoughts combined with all the other things you've put into your mind.

To hear GOD's voice clearly you need to spend consistent time in HIS WORD, there is no way around it!

HIS words to us are gentle and they do not cause us to be fearful. They are peaceful, hope-filled, right-thinking words.

They are never frantic, chaotic or confusing. They are soothing.

No matter how impatient you may be to start listening to GOD more closely, remember, everything starts in baby steps. That's just how GOD works. It's a process.

I've loved GOD passionately for a very long time, and HE's definitely led me and spoken to me many times, but in the past six years since I started spending considerable time in HIS WORD every single day, the degree to which I hear HIS voice is so much greater than it has ever been.

GOD is gentle. HE's not in a race. Learning to walk in HIS way is a process that takes time. So relax and enjoy each and every day with HIM, HE will not disappoint you!

GOD wants you to relax!

If you're anything like me and feel like your life is already a race, GOD wants you to relax.

You can still accomplish so much, probably even more than you are right now, but to do that you need to relax and enjoy HIS beautiful presence and HIS precious and personal words to you.

So, what sort of things does GOD say?

If you're not currently accustomed to hearing HIS still, small and loving voice, you might be wondering what it sounds like. What sort of things might HE say to you?

Most of the time what HE says is not earth-shattering... it's more like direction, coaching, instruction and encouragement that you need in your daily life.

So, I'm going give you a little glimpse into the sort of things HE says to me. These are just a few of the things HE said to me the day I wrote this chapter of the book, in the span of just a few hours.

I didn't make note of everything HE said, but hopefully enough to give you an idea. I will give you a little background about what I was thinking so you'll understand better: HIS words to me are in italics.

I'd been considering a new eating plan because I hadn't been eating as well as I'd like, and hadn't been exercising regularly. This had been on my mind a lot. The other day the LORD told me HE didn't want me to be afraid of food, and HE's been leading me to start eating a clean diet.

So during breakfast, while eating a bowl of oatmeal with all sorts of healthy goodies in it HE said, *"That was a very good choice, MY love."*

I always have time to think while in the shower, and while writing this book, and getting Success With GOD International off the ground, it's been a bit stressful, and the LORD keeps telling me to relax. In the shower HE said, *"Everything is exactly the way it's supposed to be."*

After showering and getting ready to leave for a few errands, HE said: *"You're doing great. Today's going to be a great day."*

As I mentioned, it's been a busy time, and I've been juggling a lot, and it's been a bit challenging at times to know how to spend my time. (Besides writing this book and launching a new company, I am still working a full time job, and have five kids living at home as well, except they're now 18-26 years old.) So, this is what HE said: *"Your book is the most important thing to focus on now. I'll take care of you at work."*

When I started stressing about something I had to do, HE said: *"So do you want to handle this on your own, or do you want ME to do it for you?"* That's what I call an "ouch-ee-wah-wah", but point well taken and I immediately relaxed and let HIM take the reins again.

Starting a new company includes many expenses, so there's a great degree of stepping out in faith, and trusting HIM going on. At the grocery store, HE lovingly told me, *"Don't be afraid to spend money."*

And as I was feeling a little guilty about even being in the grocery store because I have so many other things that need to be done as well, HE said, *"Relax, MY love, you don't realize what a major stride you made yesterday."*

All of the above took place on a Thursday morning, but it was Sunday morning when I finally typed what I wrote out longhand. And on that morning, even though I felt I had so many things to do, HE said:

"Enjoy your morning, MY love, there's plenty of time for everything!"

No wonder I'm smiling most of the time. Who wouldn't be smiling if you had that kind of companionship going on with the LORD at all times?

HE is so awesome! But the great news for you is that if this isn't the sort of conversation you have going on with HIM all the time, it can be. This is not just for me alone, or for any special group of people, it's for all of us who name JESUS as the LORD of our lives, no matter what "religion" you are, or what church you belong to (or don't belong to!)

Important note: Please keep in mind that the things HE says can also be much more specific, depending on what's going on in your life and in the lives of the people around you. This particular day was a pretty normal day without any major big decisions to make.

Immediately Obey

As the parent of five children, I can speak from experience when I say that almost nothing makes me happier than when I ask one of my kids to do something, and they actually do it, immediately!

And unfortunately, there's almost nothing quite as rare.

(Certain kids do a much better job than others!)

What's more common in my house, and maybe yours too, are comments like this:

"Why me?"

"I didn't make the mess, why should I clean it up?"

"I'm busy."

"How come you always ask me?"

"It's not fair."

"That's not my job."

"Why?" (whine, whine)

Or they say "Ok, I'll do it later" but it never happens!

But the times they do obey immediately, it's truly a beautiful thing!

It's just like that with GOD!

HE wants us to obey right away, without asking "Why?" or "What for?" or arguing with HIM because it doesn't make any sense.

HE also doesn't want us to tell HIM okay, but then not do it!

HE's looking for HIS children who will obey immediately. When we do what HE asks right away, HE knows HE can trust us with more responsibility!

Needless to say, practicing this sort of obedience involves listening intently as well. You can't even begin to obey if you don't hear HIM telling you what to do, and you can't hear HIM clearly unless you spend time in HIS WORD!

I do these things with a great level of confidence that the direction is coming from the LORD because I recognize HIS still, small voice, and because I spend significant time daily in HIS WORD, and in an attitude of prayer, worship, and companionship with HIM throughout the day, regardless of what I'm doing.

Please remember that I live a very busy life, and I know you do too. So not having enough time is not a valid excuse. We all have the same 24 hours each day, and I'm about as busy as anyone can possibly be. You don't need to spend a lot of time in HIS WORD, just make sure you get some time in each day, preferably at the beginning of your day.

As far as the companionship and attitude of worship to GOD, that's happening as I'm doing everything else a busy human being does: I have a job, I'm a mom, I'm a wife, I have five kids, I do a lot of chauffeuring, I'm writing this book and starting a new company, and YES, I still first and foremost make time to meet with GOD each and every day, and then continue that communion with HIM throughout the day.

All of this is going on throughout my normal day, and nobody even notices.

If you have a heart that is surrendered and devoted to GOD, and you're spending time in HIS Word, and in communion and companionship with HIM, and you feel HE is telling you to do something then what is most important is that you immediately obey!

HE's not trying to trick you!

HE'll never say "Oops, you missed ME, look at the mess you made now!"

No, that's not how GOD talks, and HE would never do that to you.

HE most likely sees your effort as a parent watching his baby learning to walk. Sure, the baby's going to fall, but the parent is not going to laugh at him. He's going to smile and encourage and say "way to go!"

So don't be afraid to step out! Learning to walk in immediate obedience is like working out a new muscle. At first it may feel awkward but soon it will be so natural that you won't even think about it. Immediate obedience will be your new "default setting!"

And even though it will soon be second nature to you, it will always be exciting because you never know what GOD has in store. Stepping out in faith with immediate obedience is the best feeling in the world because it really gets you in step with the LORD, and there is nothing more thrilling than that!

This past November when I knew the LORD wanted me to enroll in an expensive business coaching program, I was frustrated because I didn't have the money on hand to do it, or a line of credit to use. But I knew the LORD wanted me to do it!

It was a huge step of faith and I do not take on financial obligations lightly!

Out of obedience I enrolled, not knowing where the money was going to come from, and I had a few days to get things lined up.

HE directed me to ask two of my friends if they could help me with it. Even though it was a very difficult thing for me to do, I called each of them and asked if they could loan me the money.

Guess what they said?

Neither one was able to loan me the money.

Because of my close relationship with the LORD that didn't shake me at all. I knew the most important thing was that I obeyed and that HE definitely had my back.

The funding for the program on that day was secondary compared to this obedience test. I had such a sense of peace and GOD's blessing because I obeyed. In HIS eyes, that was the most important part of the whole deal. I knew HE would provide the resources to pay for the program. HE tests us like this all the time!

I'm happy to say that HE did give me an idea for creative financing, which included some good old fashioned hard work, and as of this date, the program is almost completely paid for.

Lots of times GOD will ask you to do something that may not seem to make sense, or you do it, but it doesn't produce the result you had hoped for.

What's most important, between you and GOD, is that you immediately obey!

GOD does that to me all the time. HE's always telling me to do things... and I always do them, regardless. I don't ask HIM a gazillion "why" or "how" questions before I act. I've learned not to overanalyze things, I just do them!

That's what GOD wants to see. HIS children trusting HIM enough to step out and do what's uncomfortable because they know HE'll take care of them.

IMPORTANT DISCLAIMER: I am in no way suggesting that you should incur a financial obligation you're unable to pay for. That is not how Christians should conduct business, ever. Period! Keeping your word and your end of the bargain as Christians is so critical. And if you sign a contract of any sort, you need to fulfill it.

> Just because GOD tells you to do something doesn't mean it will have an instant spectacular result! It's your immediate obedience to HIM that counts.

I'm convinced that all the great stories in the Bible were preceded by continual tests in immediate obedience.

We just read the really big "headliner" stories. But besides the stories we read in the Bible, I'm sure Abraham, Moses, Noah, Joshua, King David and all the heroes of the Bible were tested over and over in their obedience to GOD, and proved themselves faithful.

GOD has to test us like that so HE'll know HE can rely on us. That's when HE promotes us to higher levels!

HE wants you to be successful and to hear HIS voice clearly.

HE wants to know that when HE tells you to do something, you'll immediately obey without asking any questions.

That's the way HE prepares you for greater responsibilities. HE needs to know HE can count on you to do what HE wants.

It's a growth process. Remember, obedience is like a muscle

that gets stronger as it's used.

How wonderful and amazing it is to walk with GOD in this way!

For the eyes of the Lord move to and fro throughout the earth that HE may strongly support those whose heart is completely HIS.

2 Chronicles 16:9

I can just imagine HIS eyes moving across the world, I want HIM to see me jumping up and down waving my hands "pick me, pick me!"

What about you?

Find Your Gift and Focus

You are GOD's masterpiece.

There's no one else with your exact fingerprint, or DNA. You're one of a kind, hand designed by the Creator of the Universe, for HIS good pleasure!

There is no one on the face of the Earth with the same combination of unique gifts, talents and abilities as you. GOD hardwired you this way from before the foundation of the Earth. HE also has a very special plan that only you can fill!

You entered this world with your distinct and amazing personality, which includes the gifts GOD put inside you. Many of your gifts and abilities were undoubtedly evident to the people who watched you grow up.

It's so cool to reflect back on your childhood as a clue to what you were put on earth to do. In our home, several of my kids have gifts that were very easy to see from the time they were young.

My daughter Grace has been writing stories and books since she was two years old. Now at 17 she has proven herself to be a very gifted writer, is editor of her school newspaper and has already won many awards for her writing. She's also already a regular ghostwriter for several Internet blogs.

Ever since she was eight years old, Becky, my 22-year old daughter, has been talking about all the unusually "fancy" things she'll wear when she has her own pet grooming business. For the past fourteen years, every time we were in a store and saw a sparkly pair of shoes, or elaborate dress, we'd laugh and say that was one of the things she'd wear in her business. Sure enough, she's now grooming dogs for a living, and will one day own her own salon!

My son Josh is an amazing salesperson, and great at making profitable "deals" as far back as I can remember. In fact, the only thing we feared when we left our kids with a babysitter was that Josh might sell one of his brothers or sisters! Guess what he does for a living? He's in sales and marketing.

My son Mike has always been great with technology, IT, and

business systems and he's helped me with businesses of mine since he was eight. Mike is working in that field now and still helping me with business ventures!

As for me, one of my gifts is teaching. I've been learning things and teaching others what I've learned since I was seven years old. Back then I learned how to play the guitar, and turned around and taught all the neighborhood kids how to play. They'd come to my house and give me a dollar per lesson! Since then I've taught aerobics, dance, sales training, coaching, direct sales strategies... and now I get to teach you how to have Success With GOD!

A key to uncovering and discovering your unique gifts and talents is to take notice of something you always do, that comes naturally and easy for you, and when you do it, everything just seems to flow better... and you're energized and excited. You just feel good. It's the right fit. You do it naturally without even thinking about it! And others cannot do it so easily.

Some people are naturally artistic. Others are athletic. Some have a natural affinity for math or music. Some are mechanical, others are great speakers. Some have the gift of hospitality, and others the gift of making money.

All of these abilities come from GOD!

My husband and I had a funny experience in the Bahamas this past weekend. Although I am very clear on many of the unique gifts and talents GOD put inside me ... we both discovered one that's been there the whole time but we never recognized it for what it was. We've been witness to this gift so many times over the past 27 years together, but until this particular weekend, we didn't realize that it comes so naturally it's just about impossible to suppress.

I was asked to be one of several speakers at a Sunday morning devotional service, and had seven minutes to speak, which is not a long time. I was asked to share my testimony about GOD's role in my life, so I had to carefully prepare what I wanted to say to keep within that time limit.

The day before the event I spent time with my husband running through what was on my heart to share. The group I was to speak to were top sales professionals, all Christians. Without even realizing it, I began preparing a motivational talk about expectancy, encouraging the salespeople to believe for millions of sales, rather than hundreds of thousands of sales, with a strong call to action at the end.

My husband and I were both so excited about the message after I ran through it a few times, I'm amazed we came to our senses and remembered I was not asked to do a motivational talk for more sales, I was asked to give a testimonial about my relationship with the LORD!

When we realized what was going on, we had the biggest laugh. That's just what I do. It's how GOD wired me, and I'm unable to think mediocre and small. One of the most important reasons GOD put me on the earth is to motivate people to believe for and to achieve greater things!

Once I realized I hadn't been asked to motivate the sales team to higher sales, and that I might even ruffle a few feathers if I suggested they could double their sales, I decided to give a quick testimony and share the UPLIFT Formula to Success With GOD instead, which was received very well.

I learned something very important that day. GOD wired me to motivate and inspire people to greater things, and I always think in big terms. For me it's always millions and billions rather than thousands and tens of thousands. That is purely and simply who I am. It's impossible for me to act otherwise. I'm so used to myself and my way of thinking that it seems perfectly normal to me and up until that day I never recognized it as one of my gifts before, but now that I do, I understand the power and magnitude of the projects I take on. I was created to do BIG things, to affect millions of lives!

That's why it only makes sense that my intention for Success With GOD International is that millions of lives will be forever

> Once you discover what your unique gifts are you become much more purposeful and powerful in all you do!

changed.

It's the same for you! GOD put unique and amazing gifts and talents inside you, and you have a very important role to play in HIS overall plan! These are things you do naturally, without even thinking about it that are not easy for other people.

When you use the gifts that GOD put inside you, whatever they are, there is tremendous power in that. You can expect what you put your hands to will prosper because that's what you were put on earth to do!

There are things you do naturally without even thinking about it. It may be the gift of hospitality, organization, design, numbers, earning money, etc. When you're busy using the gifts GOD put inside you, things seem to flow and grow effortlessly, and the entire process is a great joy!

It's equally important to know what you're not gifted at so you don't waste your time! For example, I know that my gift is not figuring out technology. I can use it well enough, but to figure it out on my own is a huge waste of time. It's best for me to have someone who's good with technology show me what to do.

You may be great with numbers, but not quite as good in sales. Stick to what you're good at.

You get the idea!

Another thing that happens when you know what your gifts and talents are, and you step out and start using them, is that you feel much more powerful, and your energy level soars! You may even lose track of time because you're so involved in doing what you were meant to be doing. It's amazing.

Be careful not to compare your gifts and talents to others, though. Each and every person is necessary and has a very important part to play. GOD has equipped you for something specific, and the world is waiting for you to emerge in the power of the gifts and talents that HE hardwired you with.

If you've been banging your head against a wall, unhappy and frustrated in your career, start by adding in something you can do where you're using your gifts, you'll be amazed what happens. You'll feel fulfilled, your confidence will soar, and your personal power will emerge.

So, here are some questions that will help you identify some of your unique gifts and talents:
- What do you love to do, that when you do it or talk about it, you "light up"?
- When do you feel the most fully alive?
- What do you have the most enthusiasm towards?
- What comes easily to you that others find difficult?
- What do you enjoy doing most?
- If you didn't have to worry about earning money, how would you spend your time?
- What is something you do, that when you're doing it you get so engrossed that you lose track of time?
- If you were to write a book, what would it be about?
- If you were featured on the cover of a magazine, which would it be, and what would the article be about?

Ask some of the people around you (family, friends, co-workers, neighbors) for their feedback.
- What do they see as your two or three most prominent gifts?
- What do they notice you do effortlessly that is not so easy for others?
- What are the three words that describe you best?

Talk, Trust and Tune In to Miracles!

This is the final, and probably the most exciting step in the U.P.L.I.F.T. Formula™ for Success with GOD. This is where we do our part, and trust GOD to do HIS part. And to say HIS part is amazingly spectacular is the understatement of all times!

Remember, it's HE who:
- Holds the stars and moon in place in the sky. (Psalm 8:3)
- Put flesh on dry bones and made them come to life. (Ezekiel 37:1-9)
- Parted the Red Sea so the Israelites could cross. (Exodus 14:21-22)
- Turned the water into wine. (John 2:1-11)
- Made the sun stand still one full day to help Joshua. (Joshua 10:12-14)
- Enabled David to defeat Goliath with a single stone! (1 Samuel 17: 45:50)

And gazillions of other miracles, too numerous to even attempt to recount.

HE hasn't stopped doing miracles for HIS children, and HE certainly hasn't run out of power! HE's the same yesterday, today and forever, and HE wants to show HIMSELF strong on your behalf.

There is no telling what HE intends to do in YOUR life, but I know it's going to be AMAZING!

Now to HIM who is able to do immeasurably more than all we ask or imagine, according to HIS power that is at work within us.

Ephesians 3:20

Your role in all of this? Step out and step up!

HE's relying on you to do your part to receive and participate in these miracles. That's your role.

To love HIM so much, to trust HIM so much, to listen to HIM so intently, and to obey HIM immediately, so that your very life becomes a living testimony to HIS power and HIS love in the world today.

There are three final things you need to do to see HIS miraculous power evident in your life on a BIG and continual basis:
- Talk
- Trust
- Tune-in to miracles

From the fruit of his lips a man is filled with good things, as surely as the work of his hand rewards him!

Proverbs 12:14

Talk

Your words have incredible power, so you need to be especially careful of every single word that comes out of your mouth. Your words literally create your life! They make you who you are, and have the power to transform your life, or to keep you stuck.

In order to live a life that makes GOD proud, you should really only speak three things: the truth, according to GOD's WORD; good, positive, hopeful things (Philippians 4:8); and what you want (rather than complaints or what you don't want).

Please note that this list does not include: your problems, your fears, your worries, gossip, all the "reasons" you can't do something, your limiting beliefs, blaming others, or idle chatter.

Don't give these things power in your life! GOD's WORD says that all things work together for good; that we should have no fear of bad news; that we shouldn't worry; that we shouldn't be judgmental of others.

> The more you argue for your limitations, the more you get to keep them!

As a Christian, people you know should feel that if they come to you, you'll always have an encouraging, uplifting word for them.

I had an interesting conversation with my husband yesterday.

Time out: I have to start with a disclaimer, on behalf of my husband. It's not easy living 27 years married to me, let alone the fact that I'm a Success Coach! It's hard enough being married to anyone that long, but when one is a coach, well, you can probably imagine the conversations we have!

Anyway, we were having a discussion as we were taking a walk. Little did he know that by the time we got back in the front door, and he was at the highest point of his rant, I said, "Wait a second, hold that, I HAVE to write it down and put it in my book."

The debate was about whether or not GOD changes things "suddenly", when you have a mindset shift on something you've been struggling with for a long time. I know GOD can do that, HE's done it so many times in the Bible, in MY life, and in the lives of countless others throughout the ages, and with many people I've coached over the years.

My husband knows it's true too, he even said it to me earlier in our conversation. But when the topic turned to an area he's been struggling with for a long time, his true inner thoughts were very clear.

Here's what he said:

"The reality is that when I start seeing results I will be encouraged. I

would choose to have it happen suddenly, but what good will that do me? And how does all of this apply to someone like me anyway?"

I knew when I heard that opening line I was going to have a perfect example to put in this book. His three sentence statement contained a mixture of his default setting, a limiting belief, and an invisible brick wall all at the same time!

I'll break it down for you, just in case you didn't catch it:

"The reality is..."

Keep in mind, what he's about to say is my husband's reality, not the truth! Remember, that's what a limiting belief is!

"When I start seeing results I will be encouraged"

Yikes! I wouldn't want to claim that as the truth! I believe we need to constantly be encouraged, and encourage ourselves, way before we start seeing results, otherwise we're probably never going to see them!

"I would choose to have it happen suddenly, but what good will that do me?"

I couldn't believe what he was saying. In our household, we're all pretty in-tuned to how important and powerful the words are that we say, and Chuck normally has better self-control than to come out with a statement like that, but it came out because that's what's inside. It's a direct reflection of his "default setting" which he is working on changing. Somehow he's wired to think that everything needs to be somewhat difficult and take a long time, and that the way anything gets done is by putting in more and more hours of effort, even if there's not too much to show for it.

"How does all of this apply to someone like me anyway?"

Again, I truly couldn't believe he was saying these words, but they clearly articulated his invisible brick wall. Somehow, through whatever had been said to him in the past, he sees himself in a different category than most people, a *"someone like me"* category!

Keep in mind his response was in defense of his current position. Unfortunately these same words will keep him stuck in status quo.

Trust

The Bible is all about trusting a GOD you don't see. HE's real and HE's with you every second, you just need to trust HIM and know HE has your best interests at heart.

HE wants you to succeed and knows you're human.

HE won't let you fall!

HE's got your back!

So when you're in a situation and ask HIM to help, or have to trust that HE is helping you, even though you might not "see" what HE's up to at that moment, the more you learn to trust the LORD, the more you will be able to see HIS hand in everything!

Things won't throw you off track like they used to!

Something will happen that could be perceived as bad, but you'll have an inner peace down in your soul that it's all OK, that HE's got it under control.

> Everything is exactly as it's supposed to be!

In fact, HE often says to me "everything is exactly as it's supposed to be" even though it doesn't always appear that way through mortal eyes. Once HE says that to me, because I trust HIM so much, and stay in such close companionship with HIM, I know it's OK! I trust HIM completely!

When you live your life like this it really takes on a new dimension. You cease striving. You will live a life of unimaginable power! GOD knows your heart, and if you're doing the best you can, that's enough. HE'll pick up the slack.

Tune in to Miracles!

> *There are only two ways to live your life.*
> *One is as though nothing is a miracle.*
> *The other is as though everything is a*
> ***miracle**.*
>
> Albert Einstein

It was the week before Thanksgiving and I was on the phone with one of my dear friends. We don't see each other often and rarely speak on the phone, but whenever we do, it's always a wonderful "GOD" connection.

She owned a restaurant, and things were pretty slow. Tourist season hadn't really started yet, and to make matters worse, there was a huge construction project going on in the strip shopping center where her restaurant was located, and the project was taking way longer than she had been told. Her restaurant was lovely inside but outside was horrible due to the construction.

You couldn't even see that her restaurant was there plus the parking lot was so full of equipment and debris that you wouldn't want to park your car there!

There really wasn't anything she could do about the construction, so she did the best she could to try and get customers through her doors through advertising, great food, special events, etc.

I told her I'd pray for her and the business and did so after I got off the phone.

Just a little while later I got a call from my friend. Within minutes of me praying for her, she received an unexpected phone call that was an order for 600 Thanksgiving dinners!

I had to listen to the voicemail a couple of times and then call her back to see if I heard it right. I did hear it right: 600 Thanksgiving dinners in one phone call!

That's our Heavenly FATHER! HE takes care of HIS children, especially when HE knows that we trust HIM to do so, and that we'll acknowledge to the world that it was HIS doing!

Now some miracles may not be quite as obvious, but when you're walking in step with the LORD, tuned-in to HIM constantly, YOU WILL SEE MIRACLES, and your days will literally be filled with awe, your mouth opened wide in amazement at HIS tender loving care, and attention to even the littlest details you wouldn't think GOD would be interested in.

When you get that nudge to call someone, and you do, and you discover that they were in a crisis situation and you stepped in at just the right time with the exact encouraging word they needed to hear.

When you work wholeheartedly as unto the LORD at your job, even though you don't seem to get the results you'd hoped for, and suddenly out of the blue GOD steps in with an unexpected blessing or results you couldn't have imagined, possibly from an entirely different source.

Or when you're in the midst of a really hard day, feeling overwhelmed and stressed and GOD whispers in your ear "this is a very wonderful day" and by the end of the day you can see that too!

This happens on a daily basis, many times each and every day, when you tune into GOD!

Like the time I was in church, it was at the end of the service, and there was a lady sitting next to me that I didn't know. The LORD said, "Ask her if there's anything she needs prayer for." And even though it felt very awkward because she wasn't even looking my way, I obeyed. I told her it might sound strange, but the LORD just impressed on me to ask if there's anything I can pray with you about. She looked at me in amazement, and her eyes welled up with tears. "Yes," she said, "I have a brain tumor." And I prayed.

Or the time I was walking around the track at the park at 6 am and passed a lady wearing some sort of church t-shirt. I couldn't resist and said something to her about her shirt and the LORD. We stopped and talked, and within minutes she was telling me that she was really concerned about a health condition she had, and was going to the doctor that week. She was very scared. And I prayed for her.

A week later I was walking around the same track early in the morning and someone came running up to me. It was very odd, especially this early in the morning. It was that same woman. She just about jumped on me, put her arms around me, and gave me a big hug. She'd been to the doctor that week and he told her she was totally healed!

Or like the time I was walking into the bank, and the two people in front of me were walking slow because the man was very old. I couldn't help but overhear the man mention a Bible verse, so that was my cue!

I said "sounds like you're talking about my favorite book!" and the three of us had a brief conversation. I found out the young woman was in the midst of a serious and scary domestic violence situation, so I asked her if I could pray, and I did, and although I never saw her again, I trust GOD did protect her and her children!

That's what it means to be part of the "church". It's not what happens between four walls where everyone meets weekly on a Saturday or Sunday. It's what happens out in the world, every single day, everywhere we go!

So, in my house, it's pretty common when I walk in the door that my first words are, "I just had the most amazing GOD time!" and they can't wait to hear the story.

Please keep in mind that these things all happened because I was open to the people and the situations around me. The same is true for you.

Your part in all of this is to be so tuned into the LORD, knowing HIS heart, listening and believing HIS WORD and HIS promises to you, recognizing HIS constant gentle whispers as HE directs every single step you take.

When you do these things you begin to view everything that

happens from GOD's perspective.

You move up higher, out of the stress and chaos of daily life to a "peace that passes all understanding" (Philippians 4:7) and you will see the miracles you would have missed had you not been tuned in to the LORD.

Most days, by the time I get to my office, after the time I've spent with the LORD starting at 4 am in the WORD, then listening to Pandora radio during my shower, then more inspirational music on the way to work, I can barely contain the excitement for what HE's up to, and see HIS hand everywhere I turn!

Unplug From the Negative

Plug In to GOD

Listen Intently

Immediately Obey

Find Your Gift and Focus

Talk, Trust and Tune In to Miracles!

GET YOUR BUCKETS READY!

Now that you've learned the U.P.L.I.F.T. Formula™ to Success With GOD, what's there left to do?

Get ready to receive!

GOD wants to bless you beyond anything you've ever imagined. But if all you're hoping for is "a little old cabin in the corner of glory land" that's all you're going to get!

There couldn't be a clearer example of how important your expectancy is than the story of the widow in 2 Kings 4. As discussed in Chapter 4: Next-Level Christianity™, she was in a desperate situation, with creditors looking to take her sons as payment for her debt. To help her, the prophet Elisha told her to collect as many jars as she could, not just a few, to fill with the little bit of oil she had on hand.

> The degree to which you are willing to step up to the plate is the degree to which you will be blessed!

The oil ran out when the last jar was full!

But what if she'd gathered 20, 50, 100 or 1,000 more jars? If she had, they'd all have been filled, and not only would her needs have been met, she could have cared for an entire community!

My dear precious friend, we serve a really BIG GOD!

HE's in the multiplication business, to such a great exponential degree that it's impossible for us to fathom.

But YOU need to start thinking bigger, way bigger!

Don't believe for a $2 an hour raise, believe for double your income! (Or triple or quadruple!)

Even though right now you may be a waitress at a local café, maybe GOD would have you to be a restaurant owner!

Instead of earning an extra $500 a month in your side business, why not $5,000 a month?

It all depends on your level of expectancy.

There's a famous old poem that seems very appropriate. Even though it doesn't talk about GOD, it might as well have...

My Wage

I bargained with Life for a penny,
And Life would pay no more,
However I begged at evening
When I counted my scanty store.
For Life is a just employer,
He gives you what you ask,
But once you have set the wages,
Why, you must bear the task.
I worked for a menial's hire,
Only to learn, dismayed,
That any wage I had asked of Life,
Life would have willingly paid.
— Jessie Belle Rittenhouse

Our HEAVENLY FATHER is the KING of KINGS! And we're HIS children, and HE has an inheritance stored up for us. Our job is to receive it.

Imagine GOD's resources as vast as an ocean, and HE tells you to come and take as much water as you want.

Are you going to bring a paper cup to get your water?

Maybe a bucket?

Possibly one of those plastic pools?

Or will you figure a way to have the water piped somewhere so the supply never ends?

It's up to you! What you receive in life has everything to do with your level of expectancy.

> What you receive in life has EVERYTHING to do with your level of expectancy!

GOD's resources are unlimited, so why not get ready to receive BIG TIME?

I expect that somehow through GOD's amazing grace and mercy, and to HIS honor, that through the work at Success With GOD International, millions of lives will be changed, and one day we'll be able to say that we gave away more money than Oprah!

Why not?

Imagine all the good we can do in the world for lots and lots of people, all in the name of the LORD.

Our HEAVENLY FATHER is the KING of KINGS! HE's got all the money. We should be the richest and the most generous and selfless people on the face of the earth.

> *Eye has not seen, nor ear heard, nor has it entered into the heart of man, all the things which GOD has prepared for those who love HIM!*
>
> *1 Corinthians 2:20*

Where have you been thinking too small?
What can you believe "bigger" for?

EVERYBODY'S WATCHING!

We are walking billboards for GOD! Do you realize that?

If you are a believer, it's as if you're under a microscope, and held to a very high standard.

People are watching, they're watching everything you do!

How you conduct yourself at work, how you talk about and act toward others, how you are to strangers, what kind of tips you leave, how generous you are.

And they're making decisions about GOD based on how you live your life!

There's a whole world of people who need to know JESUS, and we really are HIS hands and feet on this earth. We are the only JESUS many people will ever see.

What an awesome honor to be representatives of the MOST HIGH GOD here on Earth.

I challenge you to live your life in such a way that Makes HIM Proud!

Mary Jo Wehniainen

STAY CONNECTED!

It's that time. You've invested several hours reading this book, and you're already starting to sense a change coming. But this is just the beginning of the road. Life with GOD is a journey that never ends, and it grows more exciting as the days go by.

GOD wants you to rise to greater levels of success and confidence in your life, and I'm here to help you do just that.

Be sure to visit me at www.CoachMJ.com and if you haven't yet watched my free 4-part mini video series "GOD Wants to Change Your Reality" sign up right away, it can change your life!

That will also put you on my email list so you'll receive valuable training tips, as well as up-to-date information on upcoming workshops and coaching programs, as well as exclusive invitations to free training events in your area..

If you'd like me to present a customized training for your employees, or speak at your church, or conduct a free phone training for your group, send an email to Info@CoachMJ.com

Mary Jo Wehniainen

ABOUT THE AUTHOR

Mary Jo Wehniainen is a professional success coach and founder of Success With GOD International.

Over the past eighteen years, she's gone from being a shy, broke, homeschooling mom to a sought after trainer and speaker.

Through her one-on-one and group coaching programs, she has helped thousands of people around the world achieve greater levels of success in their personal and professional lives than they ever dreamed possible.

A born-again Christian, Mary Jo has worked with the Christian Broadcasting Network, was recognized as one of the top 20 business builders out of 500,000 in a direct sales organization, and ran a coaching company out of her home office.

She lives in South Florida with her five kids and husband of 27 years.

Made in the USA
Columbia, SC
14 November 2018